Guess Who
Runs

Sharon Gordon

BENCHMARK BOOKS

MARSHALL CAVENDISH
NEW YORK

I am out in the field.

I live on a farm.

I like to eat grass, hay, and oats.

I chew with my big teeth.

I have short hair
on my body.

It can be many
different colors.

I have long hair on my head and neck.

It is called a *mane*.

I have four long,
strong legs.

I can run fast.

I can jump high.

My feet are called
hooves.

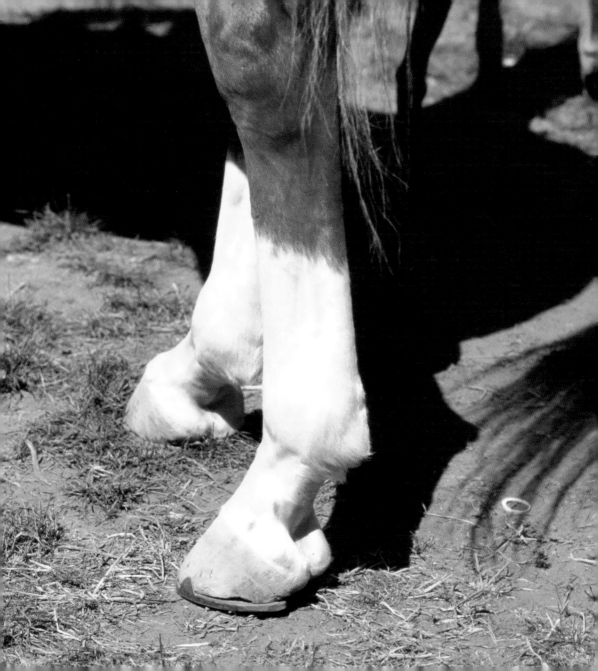

My eyes are on the sides of my head.

I can see almost all around.

I have a long tail.

It keeps flies away!

My baby is called a *foal*.

It drinks my milk.

If I get tired, I can sleep lying down.

I can even sleep standing up.

People like to pet me.

Sometimes they brush me.

You can ride on me.

Who am I?

I am a horse!

Who am I?

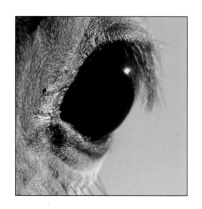

eye

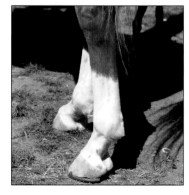

hooves

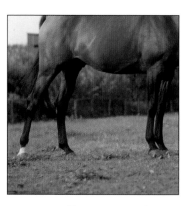

legs

mane

tail

teeth

Challenge Words

foal (FOHL)
A baby horse.

hooves (HUVZ)
The feet of a horse.

mane
The long, thick hair on a horse's neck.

Index

Page numbers in **boldface** are illustrations.

babies, 18, **19**

eating, 4
    babies, 18, **19**
eyes, 14, **15**, **28**

farm, 2, **3**
feet, 12, **13**
field, 2, **3**
flies, 16
foals, 18, **19**

hair, 6–7, **7**, **9**
    brushing, 22
hooves, 12, **13**, **28**
horse, 26, **27**

jumping, 12

legs, 10, **11**, **28**

mane, 8, **9**, **28**

people, 22–23, **23**, **25**
petting, 22, **23**

riding, 24, **25**
running, 10

seeing, 14
sleeping, 20, **21**

tail, 16, **17**, **29**
teeth, 4, **5**, **29**

About the Author

Sharon Gordon has written many books for young children. She has always worked as an editor. Sharon and her husband Bruce have three children, Douglas, Katie, and Laura, and one spoiled pooch, Samantha. They live in Midland Park, New Jersey.

With thanks to Nanci Vargus, Ed.D. and Beth Walker Gambro, reading consultants

Benchmark Books
Marshall Cavendish
99 White Plains Road
Tarrytown, New York 10591-9001
www.marshallcavendish.com

Text copyright © 2005 by Marshall Cavendish Corporation

Library of Congress Cataloging-in-Publication Data

Gordon, Sharon.
Guess who runs / by Sharon Gordon.
p. cm. — (Bookworms: Guess who)
ISBN 0-7614-1763-X
1. Horses—Juvenile literature. I. Title
II. Series: Gordon, Sharon. Bookworms: Guess who.

SF302.G67 2004
636.1—dc22
2004006869

Photo Research by Anne Burns Images

Cover Image by: *Corbis/Kit Houghton*

The photographs in this book are used with permission and through the courtesy of:
Corbis: pp. 1, 15, 28 (top l.) Craig Lovell; p. 3 Royalty Free; pp. 5, 29 (right) Dale C. Spartas;
pp. 9, 28 (bottom r.) Kit Houghton; p. 19 Kevin R. Morris; p. 21 Joseph Sohm. *Animals Animals*:
p. 7 Carol Geake. *Peter Arnold Inc.*: pp. 11, 28 (bottom l.) Franz Gorski; pp. 17, 27, 29 (left)
Fritz Prenzel. *James M. Mejuto Photography*: pp. 13, 25, 28 (top r.). *Photri*: p. 23.

Series design by Becky Terhune

Printed in China
1 3 5 6 4 2

Sept 23/16 pen on back cover notes to